A Little Book of Hours

JOHN F. DEANE was born on Achill Island in 1943. He founded Poetry Ireland – the National Poetry Society – and *The Poetry Ireland Review* in 1979. He is the author of many collections of poetry and some fiction. His poetry has been published in French, Bulgarian, Romanian, Italian and Swedish translations. John F. Deane's prose works include two novels, *In the Name of the Wolf* (Blackstaff Press, 1999), published in German translation in 2001, *Undertow* (Blackstaff Press, 2002), and two collections of short stories, *The Coffin Master* (2000) and *The Heather Fields* (2005), both from Blackstaff Press. In 1996 John F. Deane was elected Secretary-General of the European Academy of Poetry. The recipient of the O'Shaughnessy Award for Irish Poetry in 1998, and the Grand International Prize for Poetry from Romania in 2000, John F. Deane was given the prestigious Marten Toonder Award for Literature in 2001. His poems in Italian, translated by Roberto Cogo, won the 2002 Premio Internazionale di Poesia Città di Marineo for the best foreign poetry of the year. John F. Deane is a member of Aosdána.

JOHN F. DEANE

A Little Book of Hours

CARCANET

First published in Great Britain in 2008 by
Carcanet Press Limited
Alliance House
Cross Street
Manchester M2 7AQ

A CIP catalogue record for this book is available from the British Library
ISBN 978 1 85754 970 6

The publisher acknowledges financial assistance from Arts Council England

Typeset in Bembo by XL Publishing Services, Tiverton
Printed and bound in England by SRP Ltd, Exeter

Now there are varieties of gifts, but the same Spirit; and there are varieties of services, but the same Lord; and there are varieties of activities, but it is the same God who activates all of them in everyone. To each is given the manifestation of the Spirit for the common good. To one is given through the Spirit the utterance of wisdom, and to another the utterance of knowledge according to the same Spirit; to another faith by the same Spirit, to another gifts of healing by the one Spirit, to another the working of miracles, to another prophecy, to another the discernment of spirits, to another various kinds of tongues, to another the interpretation of tongues. For just as the body is one and has many members, and all the members of the body, though many, are one body, so it is with Christ. For in the one Spirit we were all baptized into one body — Jews or Greeks, slaves or free — and we were all made to drink of one Spirit.

Paul: 1 Cor; 12, 4–13

The bell doth toll for him that thinks it doth; and though it intermit again, yet from that minute that that occasion wrought upon him, he is united to God. Who casts not up his eye to the sun when it rises? but who takes off his eye from a comet when that breaks out? Who bends not his ear to any bell which upon any occasion rings? but who can remove it from that bell which is passing a piece of himself out of this world? No man is an island, entire of itself; every man is a piece of the continent, a part of the main. If a clod be washed away by the sea, Europe is the less, as well as if a promontory were, as well as if a manor of thy friend's or of thine own were: any man's death diminishes me, because I am involved in mankind, and therefore never send to know for whom the bell tolls; it tolls for thee...

John Donne

Acknowledgements

Poetry Ireland Review, *Agenda*, *Poetry Review* (UK), *Tiferet* (USA), *Harvard Review* (USA), *Field* (USA), *Body Parts* (USA), *Salamander* (USA), *Anglican Theological Review* (USA), *PN Review* (UK), *Stride Magazine* (UK), *Irish Times*, *Eddie's Own Aquarius*, *RTE Radio Sunday Miscellany*.

Several poems were published in the inaugural edition of *An Sionnach* (USA: editor David Gardiner); the sequence 'A Book of Kings' was published as a chapbook by Sudeep Sen, Aark Arts, New Delhi and some poems from the chapbook appeared in the magazine *Atlas*; 'Acolyte' was published in the collection *Manhandling the Deity* (Carcanet 2003)

The poem 'Stranger' was a prizewinner in the 2005 Peterloo Poets Competition and was published in the Peterloo booklet of that year.

Contents

The Jesus Body

Acolyte

The wildness of this night – the summer trees
ripped and letting fall their still green leaves,
and the sea battering the coast
in its huge compulsion – seems as nothing

to the midnight chime from the black tower,
reiterating that all this tumult
is but the bones of Jesus in their incarnation.
I have flown today onto the island,

our small plane tossed like jetsam on the clouds;
I watched the girl, her mutilated brain,
the father urging, how her body rocked
in unmanageable distress, her fingers

bruising a half-forgotten doll; hers, too,
the Jesus-body, the Jesus-bones. Once
in early morning, the congregation
was an old woman coughing against echoes

and a fly frantic against the high window;
the words the priest used were spoken out as if
they were frangible crystal: *hoc – est – enim –*
the Host was a sunrise out of liver-spotted hands

and I tinkled the bell with a tiny gladness;
the woman's tongue was ripped, her chin,
where I held the paten, had a growth of hairs;
her breath was fetid and the Host balanced

a moment, and fell. Acolyte I gathered
up the Deity, the perfect white of the bread
tinged where her tongue had tipped it; the
necessary God, the beautiful, the patience.

I swallowed it, taking within me
Godhead and congregation, the long obedience
of the earth's bones, and the hopeless urge
to lay my hands in solace on the world.

Gotland, Sweden

The Jesus Bones

To Market, to Market

The day was drawky, with a drawling mist
coming chill across the marshlands;
the church of Ireland stood, damp and dumpy,
crows squabbling on its crenulated stump; cattle,

that had summered in a clover field, have been herded
through plosh and muck into a lorry, have dropped
their dung of terror on slat and road. Big
heavy-skulled heads, bellowing, stretch up

over the concrete wall for one clear glimpse
of the brown fields; and what of unredeemed
suffering? What of faithfulness? Spring
they were calling out of frustrated love

for their calves, how they stood in fields,
innocent and willing, uneasy in weighted flesh
like great-aunts whose trembling long-boned hands
fumble for something in old unstitching bags.

Call Me Beautiful

Broad-shouldered, big as a labouring man, Ruth
was egg-woman, slow and inarticulate,
flat-footed in her widowhood and her big sons

slap-witted, dun as she. I was ever dumb
before her, decades of harsh news
in the lines of her face, and a small smile

grateful for neighbourly busyness; each egg,
mucous-touched, she spat on and frotted clean
against black woollen skirts. Crucifix

over the door, painted Madonna on the sill,
her house was an island on chicken-shitted ground
with a harvesting of rushes, her world

not ordered by methodical thinking. Now I know
it is my own need disturbs me, to find
meaning and motive beyond the manifest

ungainliness, to seek the spirit's dance towards
divine friendship, and to vision her rapt
on her knees in a field of corn, gleaning.

Water-Music

Sometimes I think I hear it still, the choral
symphony of ocean: bass–drum sounding
in the pounded cove, harp-music of winds

through bigfish skeletons. So much had to do
with water, for that was island, and west,
with the fickleness of rain. Weather failing

we found ourselves in manifold illusions
of otherwhere, grew angelwings on rafters
in the hayloft or gathered sheets and sweeping-brushes

to sail three-masted ships across the parlour floor.
Called to the discipline of rosary we prayed
the angels guard our souls from sin where they watched

from the four corners of our beds. When I left
gradually I misheard sea-words, sea-music among the dry
unmoving deserts of suburban nights.

But the earth lures, and at times the storms
that come hustling about the streets and stone walls
relent a little and whistle once more a casual music

with backyard timpani and the taut strings of aerials,
leaving me still with my faith and my illusions
as I walk the shores of the city, speaking praise.

Slievemore: The Abandoned Village

You park your car on a low slope
    under the graveyard wall. Always
there is a mound of fresh-turned earth, flowers
    in pottery vases. There is light, from the sea and the wide

western sky, the Atlantic's
    soft-shoe nonchalance, whistle
of kestrels from the lifting mists, furze-scents, ferns, shiverings –
    till suddenly you are aware

you have come from an inland drift of dailiness to this shock
    of island, the hugeness of its beauty
dismaying you again to consciousness. Here
    is the wind-swept, ravenous

mountainside of grief; this is the long tilted valley where famine
    came like an old and infamous flood
from the afflicting hand of God. Beyond all
    understanding. Inarticulate. And pleading.

Deserted. Of all but the wall-stones and grasses, humped
    field-rocks and lazy-beds; what was commerce and family
become passive and inert, space
    for the study of the metaphysics of humanness. You climb

grudgingly, aware of the gnawing hungers, how the light
    leans affably, the way an urchin once might have watched
from a doorway;
    you are no more than a dust-mote on the mountainside,

allowing God his spaces; you are
    watercress and sorrel, one with the praying of villagers,
one with their silence, your hands
    clenched in overcoat pockets, standing between one world

and another. It has been easier to kneel
   among the artefacts in the island graveyard, this harnessing of craft
to contain our griefs;
   here, among these wind-swept, ravenous acres

where we abandon our acceptably deceased to the mountain earth.
   In grace. In trustfulness.
This, too, the afflicting hand of God. Beyond all
   understanding. Inarticulate. Though in praise.

Towards a Conversion

There is a soft drowse on the bog today;
the slight bog-cotton scarcely stirs; for now
this could be what there is of universe, the far-off
murmuring of ocean, the rarest traffic passing, barely

audible beyond the hill. I am all attention, held
like a butterfly in sunlight, achieve, a while,
an orchid quiet, the tiny shivering of petals, the mere
energy of being. Along the cuttings

bubbles lift through black water and escape, softly,
into sunlight; this complex knotting of roots has been
an origin, and nothing new nor startling
will happen here, save the growth of sphagnum

into peat; if this is prayer, then
I have prayed. I walk over millennia, the Irish
wolf and bear, the elk and other
miracles; everywhere bog-oak roots

and ling, forever in their gentle
torsion, with all this floor a living thing, held
in the world's care, indifferent. Over everything
voraciously, the crow, a monkish body hooded

in grey, crawks its blacksod, cleansing music;
lay your flesh down here you will become
carrion-compost, sustenance for the ravening roots;
where God is, has been, and will ever be.

Seawards

In the cove, down between the echoing sea-falls,
a gull, its tawdry feathers and spread wings
bobbling in death, heaves and sinks with the waves
swayfully; the mountains and distant islands
appear to you, stranger, like clouds, like dreams;
the disconcerting land is always at your back, earth
detritus, sheep with their bedraggled wool
and a sheep-skull, teeth bared, leering into mud;
a delicate rock pool – anemone, barnacle-cluster, crab –
dotes on the danger that is ocean while the flick
of the silver underbelly of a fish warns you
of the paucity of your strivings, you, stranger,
your consciousness turning about your bones, among these
multifarious life-forms the lost one, and the saved.

Sailors-by-the-Wind

Keem Bay, Achill Island

For hours, hopeful, we rooted in the quarry
for amethyst, its flush economies, its crystals;

we found but dirt-sand, rough-stone, and the hardened
seams of peat. Till someone called, and pointed: the beach below us

was lying hushed in purpleblue, our bathing place
become a strand for seadrift, stippled;

velella velella, hymn-notes to the ocean, a myriad beached
and dainty schooners, candy floss for the rockfish,

hundreds and thousands for the cave-dark maw
of the basking shark. No man-o-war this Jack, this Tar,

its jellyfish and soft-lip-sails hoisted far-Atlantic
to the gift of tides, tacking to the winds, till the storm's upwelling

leaves them, castaway mirandas on an alien shore;
something like spring blossoms, hyacinths perhaps,

or littlenuns blushing blue under our woodland trees;
velella velella, language-boats, come blooming in their millions

over the sea's surface, invaders and non-piratical, friends
to the fat innkeeper worm, the moonjelly, the opalescent

nudibranch, pom-pom anemone, and predatory tunicate;
dry now and shivering, they lie, waiting; leaving us

wordrich in wonder, *velella velella*, while the songdance
of the oceans ebbs away from them, reluctant, at a loss.

Ass and Car

Our ageless mule
was neither one thing nor the other, not
spirit, nor all

matter. And then there was the turf-shed, its inner walls
a black-silk stipple
of turf-dust with the here-and-there

dank clot of spider-web and insect-stump; the floor
was inches deep in mould
where the donkey-cart, all paint, presided, its shafts

up-pointed. I had cart-lore then and mule-lore,
the names and functions
of winkers and collars and things; sometimes the mule,

all substance, stood
heavy with his own existence and would
not move; sometimes all jittery and wide-eyed

a sudden impulse set him
rambling, out
through the mazes of the earth and gallivanting, to halt,

stumped again and haunted, that inner light
summarily switched off. In the new age
the shed became a garage, swept, the mule

a black-sheened one-humped Morris
Minor, and all
the world was matter, dependable, and dull.

for Eva and Eoin Bourke

A Flood and Many Waters

It has rained now for days, perhaps the God
has half-decided this rabid world deserves
half-radical flooding. We have sat behind windows
watching trees darken, seeing the Canterbury bells

lose their petals to the battering. The waters of the world
begin in the dribble-drain down by the road
and the tall ships, the galleons, the quinqueremes
nudge on the hawthorn twig that goes swirling,

seawards, there. But oh! what water-music, what slick
picking of raindrops and raddle-run low-tongued roll
of the littler drums. I know, too, that the Ark
uncovered itself, in days like these, beached

on the summit of a mountain and all known life
crept out from that foul-smelling source. Once
I watched my father rise naked out of waves
and wade ashore, penis pinched small

by the cold Atlantic, the folds of his belly-flesh
wrinkling; he had followed my fishing-line
out where it was fouled on rock-weed and kelp
while I stood downcast and maladroit. Poor

son. Poor father. I remember how the rain-gusts
came stippling the surfaces and how the sea-sprat
broke in hapless foam before the mackerel shoals,
how the rain on his face gathered, and fell, like tears.

Harbour: Achill Island

The winds come rushing down the narrow sound
between islands; from the north the whole
ocean pours through, exploding against boulders,
against landfalls, and courses into quiet
when the tide brims. A seal
lifts its grey-wise head out of the current, a mackerel
shoal sets the surface sparkling as it
passes. After the storm, light across the harbour
is a denser grey, soft-tinged with green; the whip
suddenness of lightning has shone this stolid
stonework fragile for an instant and the downpour
is a chariot drawn by six roan horses
pounding in across the sea. To the eye the water's
stilled now in the bay; stones on the sea-bed
shimmer like opals, cantankerous crustaceans
side-legging across the sand. I stand
awed again that this could be the still
point of all creation, the fruits
of a crazy generosity, yet how we amble through it
as if it were our portion, and our endeavour.

Allegri

At dusk the swollen underbelly of the clouds
was a reassuring crimson; when I pray –
a new heart create in me O Lord
that the bones which you have broken may

a while, rejoice – it is to reach again
towards the music of words and the reassuring
harmonies within our sorrowing. The winds
breathing across the heathers on a hillside slope,

the baritone calls of sheep, the piccolo
sky-melodies of larks: from this rude earth I learned
the first polyphonies, while the dissonance of those
who lean on violence for their keep was a distant

rumour. May we be eased by *miserere*, knowing grief
to be the bass of elected symphonies, that Saul,
abandoned to wars and to despondency, found relief
in the soothful, soothing music of harpstrings.

in memoriam Gregory O'Donoghue

Threads

Daedalus knew, staid practical artificer,
the shortest distance between islands
is eyes down, and toes tipping the surfaces.

Over the city now snow comes, shawling
everything in old-woman grey; roofs, windows, spires
disappear with a long sigh into their wintering.

A solitary gull appears out of the gloom could be
crafted of snow; a balloon, blood-red,
its ribboned plaits dangling, lifts

optimistically, like Icarus, towards adventure.
And out of the gloom comes, too,
perhaps for reasons to do with sorrow, perhaps

the necessary onward
dragging of the day, an image of the old
silent widow, who has licked an end

of black thread, has raised the needle's eye
against failing light and will work on with distressing patience
to stitch something back into place.

The Fall

In darkening crevices between the rocks, in danger-spaces
under the erratics,
a gathering of the world's detritus: crate-bits, frayed
rope-ends, and once a canister with

Panama
stencilled, clearly still, along the side;
Killybegs fish-box splinters, dunted buoys, tin cans you could
fling on the sea

and bombard them down with stones. And once
a rosary of feathers – scuffed, some of them,
down to the naked quill –
floated at the mouth of the cove. I thought of a minor

chieftain murdered in an old war, or more banal a fisherman's
tangled and battered tackle,
until the sun set it alight a moment till it became
part of the fuselage of that young god, the bones of whose wings

were over-sensitive, wren-
soft; while the boy flew up too high the older man – dull
but wise in the limitations of flesh – did not soar; Icarus,
from up there, saw the white foam stippling

on the green-olive skin of ocean, how the land
is laid out in shades and shapes and hassocks,
and he could read
the long scribble-line of the coast. If you sit long enough

and alone at the world's margins, become
rock or spume or land's edge clod,
to the extent that you are kin
to kittiwake or crab, to rope-end or crate-bit, you will find

a momentary ease –
premonitory – how it will one day, and forever, be.

Messages to the Wind

Keem Bay, Achill Island

You come stumbling, stranger, into a world too great
for your littleness; rocks offshore, the ocean
breaking, and further out what could be tips of old
mountains, breaching, like hump-back sharks

basking. Storms off the Atlantic have laid the telegraph poles
over on their sides, like slanted sailors, flinging messages
to the winds. Midday and in the azure sky
the moon is thin as a haw upon a window-pane;

backwash of the world, salt secret and backward
sand-beach; and there she is, old lady dressed in black, asleep
in the deck-chair, her grey hair fondled by the breeze,
sea-water already reaching for her shoes. The earth, stranger,

is gentling at your feet in mythic scope and sanctity yet you
gaze only inwards with the mien of a hurt god.

A Book of Kings

I A Mere Boy

We had spent weeks
cowering in fear; this was serious, these
were the Philistines, I was likely to get hurt

fighting, our forces not being
superior. Nothing good to be expected. And then, he
stepped out from our cringing anonymity,

a mere boy. I remember
snickering. And the way
that river-stone whistled across space

like the whistle of a hawk's pouncing.
It was the thud of the great body falling
recruited me, heartily, to war;

as we cheered I could already see
the stretch of ochre sand
blushing unstoppable red; it was, you will agree,

the beginning of something, something
to rename Yahweh by, champion-maker, and champion-
killer. Slaughterer. They fled before us, a flight

of souls crying, like colonies of bats forced
into appalling light. All through darkness
the lynx and leopard, the little foxes,

gnawed on corpse and severed limb, and I could hear
hyenas cackle across the night. By dawn
I could sleep, exhilarated. I had found

David. Poet, and killer. Chosen
and perfect. Unlike me, Benjamin, big
of hand and foot, a Bedouin, a mere

boy press-ganged now to serve
Yahweh the Merciful, the Violent.
Out of accepted viciousness I try to harvest

sense: that a slight-built shepherd lad
might hear an insistent voice
urging him to attempt

impossibles. Drawing him out of dry pastures
into the marshes of blood. For too long I, too,
had scraped the desert grasses, and cursed

my skittering sheep and goats, days a slow trudge
across barren landscapes towards nowhere; I could never
get on friendly terms with the camels.

What a relief the violence! How I roared, releasing
rage I had stored up inside from years
of coaxing fires out of dried-out turds, my eyes

crossed against watching the idiocy of goats. Now
domination! Power! Bullying! What I learned
was the raucous self-proclaiming ego of the crudely giant, the more

subtle sling-shot ego of the one who would be king,
how you become a person in trampling down
the lives of others. Delicious. A mere boy

absorbed in scissoring the legs of sparrows, or a mere girl
turning her body, conscious for the first time
of another's eyes burning. Dominion! I was born

big. Large feet. A heavy head. One of my eyes
a glugger, soft-boiled. When I speak, words
solder in my throat with phlegm.

But now I stood, higher than you, and proud, at last,
of something. Empire-building with the best.
Men need, so they can swell,

enemies. Goliaths. Davids. To enemies
we can assign excess. And to ourselves
righteousness.

II *Astounded*

Saul was a bully. A depressive and depressing
lunatic. Moonman. And he was king.

David intoned a psalm before him: that straw-
gold hair, those raw–

red lips; and Saul lifted his spear
and flung it, hard. I was near

and heard it twang like a lyre-string
firm in the tent-post and David, being

fluid, like the now-you-don't-hear-it voice of God
was no longer by. I, the odd

limper, was called out of nothingness into the river's flow.
'Boy!' he called me. Jonathan. How could he know

that the word exalted me and threw me down. Jonathan, the fair,
cute-assed, white-fleshed vulnerable one. Take care,

when you have lived too long among men…
bravado, close quarters, man-smells… what I mean…

There was Jonathan. 'Boy,' he called
while he was whispering at the edge of a walled field

with David: and I doffed my cap, doffed
my brain, to the tense manipulative Yahweh, their soft

hopes that Saul might be bought, like every politic man,
though we all knew
that Saul slays his enemies by the thousands,

David by the tens of thousands, and Saul
was the less acceptable to the people!
Don't you find that astounding!

III Abigail

I began to learn the un-
tenable suffering that is bitterness:
I fell in love with Abigail.
The king was leaving, again, for his wars and ructions,

trusting me in the yard to guard her.
She was seated in the shade of a high wall,
sucking on the sweet-seed mush of figs,
juice on her lips and the dribbling of juice

on her breasts. There are wars: those
that swamp the landscape in their bruit and those
we may speak about in times of peace,
but the cold relentless wars within, and these,

have nothing at all in common. Beauty,
they say, lifts the soul to the Creator
but it cast my flesh into a stupor and overthrew me.
I watched her and she kept her eyes

turned from my unlovely form though she
could use, abuse and mortify me
and I would have uttered praise. I stood, dull
as the fig-tree suffering its heat, and would, out of rage

have torn to pieces the wildest animal to approach.
All this he knew, the poet, king, and lover.
Knew, too, my springs of enforced innocence,
my loyalty to something greater than myself.

IV Watchman on the Sand

I stand, through long nights, away from revelry,
    and have reported

that loneliness swells like a tumour; that the sun is a merlin
    lifting, and passes, circling, watchful;

that revellers cast dice for authority, their coins the mirrors
    of themselves, their laughter

speeding like knives towards the eyes of others. In truth I would
                                        report
    the rarity of peace; I would report

how reason whets itself against Yahweh's inconsistencies. I stand
    invisible, nor do you hear

my footsteps, hear only the sifting of sandgrains
    with which you build

your fortresses and ego-towers. Yet I
    am your watchman and chronicler, I report

fragments towards a conversion, I let the words
    speak for themselves as they form

shapes across the sands. I can tell how reason is a mirage – a plodding
    camel caravan

in silhouette
    on the horizon.

V *Your Name*

A warm rain falls outside, sowing its dust-motes
softly onto soft ground; I will sit here
beside you while you sleep. All my thoughts again, will be
concerning you. Your body lies
easeful, your breathing gentle as the fall of dusk.
You have gifted life and death to me
and given both your name, and with that name
I will go down proudly to my grave, my lips
holding to these exceptional words: I have lived.
The dark blue of the walls around us, here
where we have loved, will be the colour
waiting for me when I close my eyes. You

to me are truce in the long war, a tent
fixed firmly against the waging desert storm.
I will have laid the jewel of my death
in your kindly palm, or you
will have laid yours in mine, the hand
closing over it will wait, in warmth, in quietness.
They will speak of me, when they speak,
in terms of you, the way they say a stream
meanders through its chosen country. Remember
how I found you, a hurt, migrating bird
resting on a green island; remember
how we kissed, under the unblinking eye
of Mars. Here now I write your name in sand-dust
and it will blow about this favoured earth forever.

VI *Plea*

I rise today to call down blessings
on all of us who limp across the earth: all of us

stunted in brain, in bone, in fetish,
the outcasts, exiles, the never-rans,

the duck-footed, squinting, uncoordinated,
hare-lipped, back-lapped, afflicted, bald;

that we may glide with ease over supporting ice,
mercy on us, forgiveness and space in which to turn;

lessen, oh triple-handed God, the more severe
consequences of the fall, for all of us

knock-kneed, tongue-tied, botched and paralytic;
let honey flow to the joints of the catatonic

that they may spring like foals over the fields of praise;
let the dumb and foolish dribble out

secrets of the universe in their spittle and tears.
Grace oh Lord, before us, grace behind, grace

in our purposes and idleness, and let the once-and-for-all satiated
cry of release sound out at last within our dying.

VII *Bethsabee*

She was dancing, turning
through delight in her body, the water
dripping from her like raindrops from the dark
laurels, rings on her fingers

catching the *oooohs* of the sun, the bracelets
closing distance between her and the man
undone on the other roof, the heat of her nakedness
burning him brown. It was the turning time

of the year, when the thoughts of kings
veer towards war; he had carried
his swollen ego up against the sun, but in the shimmer
of the heat-haze of the day how could anybody know

what is real? He the empire-builder. King. He will make
her real. She was brought to him, and he took her, and dusk
followed, and night. A solitary, hurt,
evening star. And then, out there, the silent

predatory progress of beloved wolves, their white eyes
watchful, their long tongues
pendant. There is greed, and there are battles
always to be fought, and wars even during peacetime.

VIII   War

I have grown to abhor
all violence; I have crept, under the weight
of guilt, into the terrible Presence, only the echo
of my hesitant steps accompanying; wars
flood the earth, and ebb away, leaving
detritus, pain, and the broadcast seeds
of further wars. This is the old
threshing-floor, become the place to dare
God's holiness; only the stones of the pillars
moan in their labours, the coldness of carved stone
holding the Ark, the stone commandments, the distance
that beaten gold insists upon; I know how God
has divided himself from God, the blood of his creation
spilling on the world. David. The slaughtering
children of Israel. The innocent
crucified in thousands on the hills, in the days of harvest,
the barley being reaped. I shall beat them, sang the King,
small as the dust of the earth; and he crows out
songs of thanksgiving, Yahweh
his rock, his shield, his spear. This God? Absence being such
I call on him to walk
with hurting feet amongst us. Can this God
be born again? Can he suck affliction
from a woman's breasts? The hound's teeth
rip open the flanks of the running hare; lion cubs
feast on the pulsing flesh of the hart. That we
march, unarmed and bitter, to God's door
demanding peace. Shall man then, in his evil-
doing survive? Let Yahweh himself
know the paroxysms of pain, be
crucified, like us, be made whole again, one
God. And I see then the pietà: Yahweh-God the mother
numb and brown and dark-eyed, never having understood,
and the creature, naked, fair and cold-fleshed
laid across his knees, released at last, and bloodless.

The Downpour

The priest announced a blessing
over tuns of water; it will be measured out
in stoups where we will dip our fingers
to sprinkle drops over the clay of the world;

we will sign our bodies against crucifixion
that we might pass through into light
as sunshine glistens through a shower of rain.
It will fall over the sleeping heads

of the newly born, and on the resting crowns
of the lately dead, to wash us in and out
of this startling earth, to be an ocean
for ghost-galleons filled with souls;

to moisten, too, the long-ago dried-out bones
fallen-into-dust, the curved spine of the earth,
its knots, its cartilages, offering
deluge, purging, and sometime fruitfulness.

The Luxembourg Poem

It is May, and the bells over Walferdange
decry the struggle between gravity and grace;

in the cemetery, pansy and bluebell stand
in pewter bowls on high-sheened marble tombs

and offer their hesitant *resurrexit*, while high above
jets leave diminishing fishbone trails;

an old man, embarrassed, with knobbled
forehead and arthritic wrists, tends

loneliness with a child's green watering-can and plucks
imaginary heartsease from infertile soil;

I have been so often shifted into tears
by honey-fragrance on the air, by short-lived

extravagant blossoms of the May. In the ordered
gardens of ordered homes, stands

the final yielding of the poppies, silk-soft
petals wide-open in appeal. Rue de l'Église,

Rue de la Gare, ladies and gentlemen of old Luxembourg
tend their tired guardianship of privilege

while the rail-rhythm stay-me-not urgencies of an express
shudder the structures of clay and ossuaries in its passing.

That easy river, the Alzette, offers
no sudden kingfisher blue, nor the silver flickering

of fish, but trails its fungoid excreta, the effluent
of adolescent Europe, while out of town,

by a railroad siding, are bone-structures of abandoned
factories, with the most beautiful of weeds

flourishing in the yards and turning-places.
Yet these are the days of grace and we count them off,

gratefully, holding still with the song the robin sings
to fill the edges of the woodland – the fact

that love and light and hopefulness are burgeoning again
does not make obsolete old loves, old faithfulness.

Cemetery Sunday

They disciplined the graveyard with scythe and rake,
revealed forgotten humps and lichened stones. We stood,
each beside our properties, in attendance. This was our
groundwork of sorrow, headstones in their rows
facing towards the mountains. The priest would pass
scattering from the aspergillum a small rain
of nourishing drops. On fresher mounds, treasuries
of all-white flowers were already edged with rust.
I had cleared away, for this one hour,
trefoil, thistle, grass, I was listening for whisperings
from the turf, that spirit-flesh in its voyaging
down endless underways and spirit-passages, ghost-limbs
gliding along ghost-corridors and pitying us, perhaps,
who stood solemn in the earthen vessels of our flesh.

Mapping the Sky

These sharp nights you might see them – lines
etched in silver pencil between the stars, wide
family tree with names and dates and histories –
or skeletons in a dance so fast you scarcely
notice movement – a child's mobile where she lies
on her back in the cot, fingers and toes in an ecstasy
of mimicry. I, too, would dance if I could riddle
flesh sufficiently to find the source, make
feathers of my bones, to be with the clean birds
circling, and murderous. Now I must step indoors
from the cold to listen to the winds swing
caustic down the chimney, while the old and wise
pray for sailors out tonight on the wild seas,
for right balancing, for knowledge of the one star.

Mappa Mundi

Let this then be your diary and yearbook: make
    a frame of oak on which to fix
a sheet of finest vellum, stretched, like skin; draw

freehand, a not quite perfect circle; use black
    ink, some red, for the heart, let's say, for the Red
Sea; blue for rivers, veins; brown-egg shapes

for mountain ranges, and for faith; focus it all
    towards the centre, Christ, his bones stretched wide
in crucifixion, colour him too insistent red

to confute the non-believers. Puce, for wars, but let it not
    predominate. Have angels of the agony above
and devils snarling, scarlet, in the guts. Remember

that something within the frame of bones grows wiser
    as the bones grow heavier, the same that shifts
your being gratefully towards cessation. Now see

how down the long avenue the cherry trees once more
    have siphoned all the juices of the earth
into extravagant blossoming, a canopy for wedding feasts, a Bach

cantata in the key of white, but in you, memory –
    or the doleful rhythms of experience – hold the heart
from lifting in exultation, chill winds being possible

and unseasonable frosts. Remember, too, how the monks
    laboured years over their charts, finding in the corners
place for monsters, for the slithery ladder and the sulphur

lakes beneath. If there is time, etch in gold leaf your fabled places,
    Samarkand and Valparaiso, the pancreas, the afterlife.
Something within the frame of bones is in no rush

to clothe again the hard-won nakedness of spirit. Fig-leaf. Rue.
　　When you are done, step back, and gaze awhile
into the mirror, note contour-lines about your face

and the curious light still shining in your eyes.

The Jesus Bones

It was full summer and the skylarks soared
over the wild meadow;
across ditch and hedgerow the dog rose draped
its flesh-pink shawl while the flowering brambles reached

dangerous fingers
towards the flowerbeds. A bat lay dead on the garage
window-ledge, amongst webs
and husks; it was curled up tight, perfect as a babyfist

though flies already
had laid their eggs in the sacred caverns of the ears;
I touched the fur and brushed the unresisting skin of night.
The holly leaves were hymning in the sun

and small birds flitted through them;
it, too, was shaping in torsion – subject to corruption – a green
promise of clusters of the most scarlet of all berries; tree, I imagined,
of the knowledge of good and evil, its bitter roots

driving into the humus of our sleep. I would be, at times,
animal, thread of the skein of earth, free
of the need of redemption. Once I crept along a ditchtop,
in a tunnel of rhododendron, on earth mould,

leaf mould, on blossom-droppings, the tiny hardnesses
stippling palms, and knees;
this was everyday adventure,
the eyes of blackbirds following and their alarm calls,

with the strange and beetly
insects frightening me, their throbbing, their pebble-eyes.
I could fall silent there, hidden on the pulsebeat of the earth, mind
vacant, body stilled. Part of it. To receive.

And watched the fox slip by the drain outside,
there, uncareful, in daylight,
each russet hair sun-burnished, the breathfilled brush
like an old guardianship, a queen's train, that sorrowing eye

rounded, where a moon-sliver shape of white
startled me; her long tongue lolling, the teeth were visible
in a grim fox-smile. My breathing stopped and a tiny shiver of
fellowship
touched my spine. A moment, merely. Then

she was gone. A magpie
smattered noisily in the trees: *one for gloria, for hosanna.* If, in our
waking,
we could mould it all into a shape, beautiful and at peace
the way the electrically burnt heart of Jesus

found rest in the rock tomb
though we are many, seam and femur, root-system,
belly, spleen. Night, and the moon dressed the storm-black clouds
in scarves of buttermilk-white while a solitary star, as if hastening, sat

over the eucalyptus tree. We –
not animal enough and cruel beyond thought –
go scattering blood over the earth
as we might scatter water off our fingers,

big-headed man, articulate, stitching and unstitching
mindlessly as we pass. The Jesus bones
have been nailed into the timber of the tree, the blood
in its revolutions

pouring through the puncture-holes, this man,
of localised importance, this Jesus-fox, who broiled fine fish
on a nest of stones by the lakeshore; this
rag-and-bone man, this stranger, this lover, giver, priest.

The Jesus Body, the Jesus Bones

Invocation

Raindrops hang from the black branches
of the rowan; snowdrops, those froward maidens, stand
in small, lisping groups; it has always been a question
of our waiting, of our stooped labouring; send

your angels, Lord, so they may moult over our walkways,
snowstorms of cherry-blossoms lightening
our gutters. I would be, even once, a Saul
to encounter you, be felled, blinded, only to rise

with the burden of a different name. I live,
sometimes attending, sometimes distraught,
knowing you will not step from shadows, disturbing
form, but may swell within me like a tumour, fraught,

halting me, and frightening. That at least
your presence be insistent, like frost-skreeks, like stones
and bird-song, that you endow me with the hard
muscle of will, and with patience, its thin taut bones.

A Little Book of Hours

I lay my life out before you, a fading
many-folded and torn map, to see if you
figure there, or how. Innumerable
words and gestures, the going down
of sun and loved ones, and all the regular returns,
journeys through the under-ways of cities and out
high roads along the cliffs – all that goes to print
an individual living, I lay them out in scarved
irregular patchwork, grid-numbers; reference-points.
I trace my finger on line and fold and contour
and find you nowhere, and everywhere, the very way
I cannot point to any moment that is I, wholly
and essentially, and yet in every moment it is
you, and I, wholly and essentially, and unknown.

Villa Waldberta, Feldafing; Germany

★

The distance between us has been islands –
imagination, open country – in its time and place
insisting; the distance between us
has been days, hurrying to years, has been this
struggling under burdens, of the body's weight, the spirit's
urgings, has been limb-pains, anguish, how the flesh
slackens and grows weak; the distance
is from here back to islands, to daffodil-
days of imagination, the mind open to receive.
The distance between us is my living; and my death.

Lipica, Slovenia

I

Where the journey begins. A point of stillness
under a limewashed wall, weak sunshine, the blind man –

a rug across his knees – seated on a rickety, motionless
rocking-chair; sounds of wren and sparrow from the whitethorn
hedge.

Without a future. His observance of the ways of goodness
has made him enemies; he had escaped, once, from the wrath

of politicians and existed, in Birmingham, in exile. That
was then; now, allowing the present, he can see how he is

nothing. Therefore forgiven. And, in stillness, innocent. Warm
day, out of season; magpies chafing on the bare trees

like omened fruits, squabbling over spring, the reproductive
wars. Last autumn's remnant leaves, frayed and threadbare,

have been blown into the hallway. Stretched at his feet
'Tobit', old mongrel, head on his paws, wearied by long life,

pus from his eyes, his body slowed arthritic. Beyond,
along the median, a march of drindling daffodils, blown

by motorway dust and the blear of exhausts; while, in the dark
of a curio room under the stairs, fishing rods have been

folded away, coloured baits in their boxes, reels, and lines. He is
nothing, waiting on time. Still. The journey is begining.

Bunnacurry, Achill Island

i

When I was small enough I rode
the banisters down their smooth slope; you
were not there, you were irrelevant;
when I was small enough the world itself
was wonderment, down the flagged hallway
to the kitchen door. Night I could hide
when I was small enough, on the third step
to savour the murmuring and laughter
from the parlour, a string of light under the door
focusing comfort; I was imagining
the turf fire, light on sherry glasses,
the sheen on the shut lid of the piano,
imagining coins, cards being shuffled –
till I slept on the stairs and cried in my sleep
and was lifted, still small enough, back up to bed.

Bunnacurry, Achill Island

⋆

With a quencher long as a billiard cue
raised to the six high candles, I swung
my starched-white surplice and sent fragrant ghosts
whispering amongst the rafters. Light,
coloured whey and honey and cobalt, played on the wall
through the simplest of stained windows, and soon
only dust-motes across the light were left, and I, acolyte,
born to it, competent and indifferent.
I was gangly then, slow-witted, willing,
and you were playing games around my ignorance,
wheedling me already through my senses till you kindled
a small indigenous flame within me, to become
spur, and irritant, un-
quenchable, immediate, un-pure.

★

With a stump of white chalk,
a squared-off piece of black slate,
I inscribed, to perfection, the word
GOD. I remember concentration, teeth
irritating against the lips, harsh
scraping sounds as I worked. Remember, too,
no words of praise or acclamation but only
small clouds of dust rising as I erased.

Bunnacurry National School

★

I was taught your laws from my first days,
how love equals obedience, Scots pine in the grove
standing firm, wind off the hills
scarifying the lake, Nanna's fingers raw
from a washing rock at the lake's edge. All else
the hopeful ways of pilgrimage, the undefined
distances and teasing of the names: Zebulon, Naphtali,
the fabulous disasters of your stopping-places.
Sometimes you lazed among the kitchen scents, Nanna
in a whirlwind of flour, in the range the swelling
of soda farl, potato bread or rhubarb pie. Granddad
as if he were always setting out, consulting
an old fob-watch, ticking you off, his evening
a ritual of lamp and pipe, advice and prayers, and she
concerned more with food for the journey, with comforts, care.

★

You do not answer or if you do
I have not yet learned the language. Grey
these hours, this half-motivated gloom, the heart
hung for a time in unthinking emptiness. You
soaked me once with rain, a long chilled afternoon,
the sea off Achill rough, uncompromising. I sat on rocks
over a cove, heavy myself as rocks – I sought
some rope of the imagination to tie me to you,
some glimmering of light beyond the dark that all
our love and striving, the long and unwilled
suffering of flesh, might somehow be a little more
than the unwilled suffering of flesh, but you left me
cold and bitter, rain coming in sweeps across the rocks
and ocean battering itself along the coast, lost things
tossed in febrile pointlessness in the cove.

Dooagh, Achill Island

ii

You were not here. It was a question then
of getting through. You were not to be encountered
here. Far from islands. Walls only. A huge
house I saw as prison. Lessons and routines.
The dulling round. The lift and freedom
I associate with air and sea and mountain ruck
utterly absent. Elements to rhetoric. Rudiments
to grammar. And you grown part
of algebra, of trigonometry, of dead
languages. Once each term we spoke, you and I
throwing our arms in the air in glorious release –
Te Deum Laudamus. And I was already back:
Manulla Junction, Westport, Achill Sound...
to real and beautiful, the real, the beautiful, and you.

Mungret College S.J., Limerick

One early summer evening I stood in the abandoned
college field, goalposts white and still, like footmen
left with no one to wait upon, and the air replete
with thrushes' songs, something young and independent
yielded in me, something passed in the dusk above me
ruffling my hair and I was taken by incorrigible sorrow –
perhaps to do with endings, with my first affect
of lonesomeness and I knew, standing away at the field's edge,
hands in my trouser pockets and suitcase packed for home,
I would seek you out by name and knowledge, you
already chalk in my ignorant bones, already
unknown erratic in my untried flesh.

Mungret College S.J., Limerick

II

To be young, and setting out, Tobit in his excitement crazed,
sniffing at the new world. The boy

given a purpose; down from the bridge, down
concrete steps, by the riverside path. It is the future that attracts,

the path turning in the distance into intriguing woods, and in the end
the bargain, sealed; then the return, the path turning in the distance

into intriguing woods, then other purposes, and others. At the first
turn

the companion waiting, geared for the journey. Mallard

swimming in pairs, skittish; a swan stomping the bank
with proprietorial authority. The accompanying

angel beautiful; rucksack packed, the young moustache
fair and strawlight, but the stride purposeful. Three men,

grubby, a little menacing, are slurping beer from cans
under the crumbling factory wall; a magpie

picks at something in the grass; the companion,
will be forever there as shadow and as light

with promises. The young man, too, makes young-man promises.
They move on. The river moves. Day moves on. The river moves.

Newport, Co. Mayo

i

Here, I thought, is where you must be,
this inland island, hospitium of trees and shrubbery,
low hills and heathland walks, blackbirds and silence; here
I will find you, God Incarnate, you mattering, the matter
beautiful. There was a high and curved conservatory,
exotic flowers rising among palm trees
out of a hot-tub undergrowth of luscious greens,
a pond with crimson fish and a bronze heron, a fountain
whispering constantly your name. I see it now
as your snare of loveliness, and I a bee
lured into the orchid cave for nectar; trapped.
But oh how I would love you, how I would tread
track and path and highway that the ministers of your care
would point to, I would become a spirit-bird
lifting from the earth into your close.

Novitiate, Kilshane; Co. Tipperary

★

Here was the medieval larder of sweet
forbidden things. For now
see me, regulator, and keyed. My room
apart, my personal alarm, *laudetur*
Jesus Christus. Pre-dawn, in darkness, I move,
embodied spiritan, down unlit corridors, sure of you,
solitary, like you, though among peers, a never understood
impulse holding me, in the prescribed place
at the prescribed time. I am functioning as bell-
ringer, cock-crower, my brothers' keeper.
By rule and regulation every breath I take
gives glory to my God; I wear God's smell
and carry on my person the darkness of my God;
matins, before the thrush or coal-tit, until night's
soothing psalms of compline before owl or bat
loom or squeak – I regulate: am
regulated: pray: am prayer. *In aeternum. Amen.*

Novitiate, Kilshane; Co. Tipperary

★

I set to study you, your dealings
with the Fathers, theirs with you; the frayed
recital of adventures of your Don Quixote saints. I sat absorbed
in a long low building, like the country dance-halls
my peers were louching in. All my concentration
was on you; the dry black figures of my superiors
moved like stone statues and all was medieval, silent and obtuse;
I learned another language in which to speak to you and knew
certainties and happiness and a many-layered security.
Love was the word reiterated everywhere and I could
decline it: *amor, amoris…* my body held
and cinctured, my spirit burning, *ignis fatuus.*

Novitiate, Kilshane; Co. Tipperary

ii

It was the music then that lifted me –
male voices raised into the sacred chant,
a wood of poplars blown this way by the breeze
then that, following rites the way the poplars yield
to necessary force; Gregorian, the long-drawn
alleluias, the essential harmonies of Palestrina,
the flow of antiphon and responsorial; so many of us
a fair field, surpliced and in choir, and I imagined
you sitting in your comfort chair, eyes closed
and hands resting across your paunch, delighting in it,
dispensing grace and glory to us privileged –
though now I know it was my own elated being
relishing the music and relishing it
mostly beyond your listening.

Seminary, Kimmage Manor; Dublin

★

At night, in my small cell, the world beyond
bathed in silence under an eloquent moon, I lay
sleepless, breathing a loneliness not spoken of
in the texts, and though intelligent of the ordered
mechanisms of your universe, in my own soul
disorder swelled and I found
nothing in mind or body that would answer
questions I could not find the words to frame.

Seminary, Kimmage Manor; Dublin

★

Mid-morning, when the others were at Lauds,
I crept away, a small suitcase in my hand,
down the marble stairway and out beneath yew trees
to wait, under the high wall, for a bus
into the city. I see it, not as failure, but as your way
of weaning me from poesies of the island
to the dry mathematics of your concerns. I was welcomed
home. Strange place. Strange comforts. A stranger
on the bleak island of the world and in its rhythms
you faded to a dim, a medieval legend. Still
I walk these shores a stranger, my gaze
wandering out over the ocean, caught again
by the mysteries of kittiwake, puffin, auk.

Dublin, and the World

III

He stands under black arches of the bridge; below the bridge
the pool, its slither-movements down in darkness;

reeds near the lower bank, warblers restless and cheeping;
and near the reeds the carcass of a full-grown dog, sack-

ugly in the water, and stinking; black water, holding, and cold.
On the higher bank a gruntled ditch, with nature's

inherent harmonies, violet and primrose and wild strawberry;
on mayblossom thorn a blackbird is shaking his body in rage

and bluebells preen in secret gardens among the weeds.
Sometimes his prayers are fists, beating themselves to blood

against a door that is not there, and scared that it may open
to admit him; sometimes his prayer

is the whispering high-pitched call of the goldfinch
greeting sunlight through the pines. Suddenly the may-fly,

storm of snowflakes over trout and pike in their frenzy.

Dodder River, Dublin

i

On a dark night I found her;
I offered her a flower-heavy branch of haw, the thorns
not troubling; it would be
happiness for ever. In your care. And blessed.
We woke, years later, to the blood
that was not right within her, to pain reducing her
to an object of pity and of terror. Though
beautiful. Your care
alloyed with sorrowing, with the way our small
strengths fail against the brute
mechanisms of your glory, till I came
to curse you, to cry against the God who could
riddle what is beautiful
with barbs of intolerable suffering and I lost
her, and lost
you whom I'd served, decade upon decade upon decade.

Riversdale Grove, Dublin

★

She whom I loved
was whispering secrets to her death.
She had embraced
suffering and left me pathless
beyond her door.
What could I do but pray – *please*
take her gently from the world.
She whom I loved was not
she whom I loved. I stood
beyond the door and beyond the door
was nothingness and nothingness
had her in its embrace and you
were nothingness. She stopped
whispering then and her climax
came without breath.

St. Vincent's Hospital, Dublin

ii

Fields of thistles and scutch grass stretched away
behind the house, cowpats, like patches of disease,
on its green skin; sloblands of the river by the ditch,
suppuration of the mud, stench of things decayed,
predations of stilted birds across low tides.
I let green things grow, unchecked. I was aware
of cattle in the fields at dusk plodding towards a gate.
You scuffled to enter in my poems.

Mornington, Co Meath

★

I watched them coming out of church or house,
their fingers tipping absently in the blessed font
and scattering a tiny mist of water on their flesh
and on the sacred threshold. A cleansing,
of the earth and of the person. Though inadequate.
I saw a coffin, the grained wood sheened and stained
to enviable beauty; as it was carried out, a small
spattering of water, and the drops
clung to the polished surfaces. I thought of trees,
how they had gossiped heartily under the gifts
of rains. Of water. Holy. And how the priest
sprinkled moisture in from a plastic bottle, his black
soutane feathered in the bitter wind, and the wood planted
again in the bleakest earth. And watered. Now
when I stand in the comfort of trees and under rain
an overwhelming lonesomeness will take me and I watch
furtively away among the darkening boles of the woods.

Walferdange, Luxembourg

IV

Now the wild meadow is swollen in exuberance,
orchid, self-heal and maidenhair, the blood clover and the milk.

Noon, the bedroom, lace curtains frisky at the open window;
days of hesitation, of a wariness before flesh, until at last

the little death, explosion of seeds into the fluids, swimming
towards life. Scents of honeyed fruitfulness, though candles

on the chestnut trees were already burning out. Night, then,
this the dream and how it swells to nightmare:

an old house among trees, a stagnant
swimming-pool; in dusk light he falls

into viscous water, he is clothed, prepared to scrabble but his feet
kick against something, something shifting and soft, a decay

underneath that will soon
encompass him, viscous arms gripping him about, it is

Asmodeus, demon of savagery and despair, and he flails
uselessly, screams clotted in his throat, till he wakes

wet and sweating, and holds, in grief, to the peace
of her presence, whom he will wish to love forever.

Sandymount, Dublin

i

The strand: the tide so far out it is a line
drawn by a silver pencil on the horizon; I walk
under a grey sky by tide-pools and gullies, ridges of a hard
sand; I stand in the centre of a great bowl, on three sides
the living city, on the fourth the sea; extraordinary lives
delve in the sand about me; black-back gulls are harsh
at my intrusion; I have found love again
and am amazed at a life's new energies. Distance myself
from my own amazement to seek you out in the local
temporary desert; but find instead the spectacular fall of a tern,
a huge ship on the horizon shimmering in mirage, a far
bass-organ fugue from the city's engines and a throb of life
shivering again through my blood.

Sandymount Strand, Dublin

★

The river takes its natural turns and twists,
the road follows, impelled to. And she
who wrote God down for me in weights and measures,
is at the head now of a slow and dark procession
wending the road that wends with the river; black
hearse, black stream, that will come soon to a halt
by high walls, under high trees. Mother. Love
was a word rarely uttered, her strong heart
battling ever upstream towards a source, all restful pools
to be eschewed. Lies now in your care; teach her
love; who taught me; and teach me, you; wrap her
in arms of unstinting spiritual sensuality that her firm soul
yield, that the love I was unable to offer her
impel her at last into ease of the great ocean.

Bunclody, Co. Wexford

V

Light glints off the railway tracks; a lemon butterfly has come to rest
waiting for the throb and shuddering of an approach; late

summer dust, premonitory coughing. Now is the time,
when he has settled to contentment, to set out again;

another airport lounge, a whiskey, the nail scissors
in his washbag setting off alarms... Before they lose him

father and mother call him home. In the strange city the river,
flowing north, is forced to pass through restraining walls:

curving and deep under the fortress, branched and wider
under the grey historic bridge; it sings a terrible music here

how down the centuries men's murderous blood runs hot;
unheard now through tourist calls, the jazz bands, beggars,

the petty thieves and caterwaulers, loudhailing guides…
Chill winds already begin to shiver the restaurant canopies

and quench the terrace candles; from distant hills
summer waste already flows, sere and sodden, thickening

the water, shaking the stalls, caricaturists, whores,
who wrap themselves away each evening earlier. He, impelled to,

presses on, prayers the stones he flings
to skim across the water's surfaces, towards you.

Prague, Czech Republic

i

Morning, strange city; people hurrying by
outside; a chainsaw starts, screams and dies;
I am disturbed by the unfamiliar; women come
to strip the bed of sheets, the room of towels; I feign
unconcern, but long for home already, try
to pray; a wheelbarrow, below the window, tumbles
spades and picks and shovels in a harsh chord
out over the pavement. Ultimately, I know, it is you
I strain for, beyond this room, this day, beyond
rooms and days; a closure; rest. Doors bang
in a foreign language; there's a lukewarm
stew of radio-music; and this is how we live, as blind men
groping for your kindly, unsettling hand?

Lyons, France

★

Take your pen, you urge, and write: God.
But I resist and write
sea-mew; fuchsia; city; moon.
You insist, write: God. I say —
I have no pen now, I use PCs.
Then type out: God, you say, translate me
into this your century.
I type out: God; and then delete, type
sea-mew; fuchsia; city; moon.
And when I hear you laugh I know again
you are the letters of every word I use, you
the source and form of every poem. But,
I plead, the people mock and say that God
is not fit subject for our century. So I write once more
sea-mew, fuchsia, city, moon. And you say
yes! you have written me down again.

Everywhere

ii

The moon, host-white and cold, holds tonight
in my window; often when I pray you hear
only the noise and embarrassment of words,
though I would lay my life down in trust,
emptied of will, attentive. The winter fields
are scutched and water-logged; plover
lift together and wheel, and wheel again as one,
following an inner impulse, their underwings
pale a moment in grey light on the fields
then dark once more. Hedgerows stand shorn
in military fashion, waiting, I can see through them
to the other side of things. The moon
holds in my window and if I slip meanwhile
into silence you in your absence answer me,
an inner impulse quieting. Days and nights
the river through the suburbs has been in spate

cold-coffee-coloured, the lower branches stained
with banalities of man's passing; a swan,
ousted, grey-soused, stravaiging, comes proudly
down the median, its high neck challenging, and evening
traffic stalls, fuming again, incapable.

Rathfarnham, Dublin

VI

Already the sea makes roads this far inland,
the river scurrying to hold its individual name,

banks darkened by tidal excreta; the crushed beer cans
bobbling under falls are held in restlessness;

the chasuble the earth wears in earliest spring
is bitter lemon; now it is ashen-grey, leaning towards black.

Remember the old man left resting in the sun? He
is dead now, and is calling home his son. There will be stillness

in the garden, the old bench falling sideways; and no dog
curls itself up to dream on the ravaged lawn.

Cypress Downs, Dublin

i

Ah my dear – I have come to rest on this
well-arranged and fancifully-named estate, this arabesque
outpost of the city, its laid-out cloistral culs de sac,
the urban high-tide waves touching against its shores;
if I have settled to contentment, I ask myself the more
about your presences, your absence. The seasons here
are marked by cards at the newsagents; magpies
rule the roosts; marauding cats scrape faeces into earth
we have hauled home from a garden centre; I do not
mock it; it is holding ground for our awkward children,
an island we have stepped out on for a while
from the grander voyage. We are assiduous
about what we conceive as beauty: ionic columns, hang-
ing flower-baskets, ornamental shrubs, and then within
our fragranced candles, holiday souvenirs, our standard lamps.
Am I then pusillanimous, as always, shielding my small light
against the storms, touching you briefly to ascertain
if you, or I, still live, offering my poetry to you and to
the hard disc of my computer, wondering which of you
receives them better, retains them, and grows warm.

The Heath, Dublin

★

I murmur a heartfelt sorrow for offending you: the sin
is ongoing, disintegration, acceleration towards
the grave, original evil, for which I am, and will remain,
always heartily sorry. I reach from the whirling rim
in towards the axle of calm. If I pray
that you should throw me down, confound
my caution, I fear the more that you might
answer. My wrestling has been with
myself. Your absence, your unreplying shade, refusal
to give yourself a name, I resent; my reasoning
not being your reasoning, my purposes not your

purposiveness. If you throw me to the dust I fear
I might rise, like Paul, though injured, and lose
the comfort of my half-heart, and the safe
distance I may still keep, from you.

Everywhere

VII

How the old blind father and the old stooped mother
held each other's dried-out flesh in extended stillness

and melted back into one another, into death, knowing
a last orgasm. He has journeyed with the angel; he is not

alone now: she whom he has found is with him, she and he
hold to each other's flesh in extended stillness, watching

their children leave, one by one, happily, and waving back.
That warmth in the late sun caressing the shoulder-blade:

stillness of cut iris in the glass bowl, the quietness: is this
the angel? has he gone to rest somewhere inside the body?

has he been recalled? Slip words now in to the small interstices
in time's spokes, to stop the blurring long enough, to see.

Villa Waldberta, Feldafing; Germany

★

Seagulls litter the grass in the city park, a crowd
gathering for a rockfest; there's an arctic
wind blowing in on them though a hardy few,
hovering almost kestrel-wise, test the buoyancy;
the silvering black of rooks startles amongst them,
their aggressive stomping, their perk. They feed
on something, yet all that sings across my mind
are words out of our shorn past, years we thought
you more violently cruel than we wanted to believe,
your just and chastening hand; and still I cry
deep in the unsounding chasm of my soul, out
of the depths. My heart buoyant at times, at times
blistering like the suffering souls. The gulls
lift together suddenly, shifted by a japping dog
and wheel away as one, crowding the sky with silence.

Cold Comforting

Satan, they admonished me, can fork you deep
    into Hell's hot gurgitating belly
but all I garnered from their words was an interest
    in the ashpit, that slumped and breathing
presence against the backyard wall. Waste
    from the Aga, from the parlour fire,
turf-ash and wood-dust, with the sizzled-out strings
    of bacon rind and the charred heads
of fish; with all the burnt secrecies, detritus
    of our hiding-places and ducked habits, and she
– old grandmother whom I loved –
    dragged sideways by the blackened bucket, ash-motes
lifting in the breeze and loafing
    about the shrubs and gateways. Still
something of the brute indifference of fire
    irked me, the obduracy
of insentient things and how I could not trade soul-secrets
    with pine or snipe or beetle. The Devil, too,
is of the Sons of God, has taken out
    leasehold on the world, determining
slug and butterfly, the dailigone yielding of the flesh
    to sorrow and decrepitude. We are all,
she told me, of the Daughters and Sons of God, rooting
    among the silks and sicknesses of ash
for more than silks and sicknesses, for Leviathan, the lost
    glory of our purposes, for Behemoth,
the impetuous urgencies of love.

Tracks

I was carried in from the shore of eternity
scarcely the length of a snipe's flight
from the asphodel meadow; I would go down
into the embrace of clay

testing the haphazard richness
of flag and fern, of cress in the waterlogged hollows
and extravagant dragonflies darting like thoughts
from frond to thorn;

at home you could hear
the turf-sods as they whispered to themselves
of their own, far-distant past; in the delicious fear
the fireside yarns offered

we heard the oil-lamp's tongue
tsk tsk against the globe; half-whispered tales
of the devil's hoofprint on the yellow lane, of bodiless
hooded shapes that passed

moaning across the dusk; though soon
this lore began to moulder into wisdom and the Christ's
careful footsteps we would follow through straiter ways.
The meadow waits

not far from the ungovernable sea
where my mind finds rest, imagination comfort; let them say
he is not here, he has gone rambling again by the shore
where the black hag flies, and his Christ.

The Poem of the Goldfinch

Write, came the persistent whisperings, a poem
on the mendacities of war. So I found shade
under the humming eucalyptus, and sat,
patienting. Thistle-seeds blew about on a soft breeze,
a brown-gold butterfly was shivering on a fallen
ripe-flesh plum. Write your dream, said Love, of the total
abolition of war. Vivaldi, I wrote, the four
seasons. Silence, a while, save for the goldfinch
swittering in the higher branches, *sweet*, they sounded,
sweet-wit, wit-wit, wit-sweet. I breathed
scarcely, listening. Love bade me write but my hand
held over the paper; tell them you, I said,
they will not hear me. A goldfinch swooped,
sifting for seeds; I revelled in its colouring, such
scarlets and yellows, such tawny, a patterning
the creator himself must have envisioned, doodling
that gold-flash and Hopkins-feathered loveliness. Please
write, Love said, though less insistently. Spirit, I answered,
that moved out once on chaos... No, said Love,
and I said Michelangelo, Van Gogh. No, write
for them the poem of the goldfinch and the whole
earth singing, so I set myself down to the task.

Lucy in the Sky

They have gone down into old earth
to prepare their motorways and have discovered

bones; yellow big-engines with their jaws and angers
move in sway-time on a scaffolding of skulls; like sods

of dried-out turf, the scapulas of biped hominids
are unearthed; what makes us human, we are told, is laughter

and walking upright. Pithecus, and Peking Man Erectus,
and they found Lucy, of Ethiopia, one forearm bone

reaching from the soil, forty per cent of her
raised skywards in tentative resurrection. And you, the Christ,

they raised you skywards and hammered you in,
bones stretched and shattered on the hill of skulls,

they put you under earth where we, too, marginalia,
will lay us down inside the calcium honeycombs, longside

the Jesus body, the Jesus bones, resurrections that a slight
contemporary breeze might whisk out of our seeing.

Set Lucy upright, cautiously, dust out the orifices of heard
melodies, of sand-marrow; clean between the teeth

and snuff dust out from the nostrils; think of eyes that have absorbed
the light of summers, of a brain that has stored truths and trivia,

language and languages and a modicum of history. You will find
nothing of that. Dust carefully the bones; perhaps the Christ

has already raked them through, rifling what's left
for garnered treasures. Take care, too, with the skull, the jaw askew

in mocking laughter. Who she was, or is, or if she watches still,
she is indifferent to your amorous tickling of her bones.

Kane's Lane

The substance of the being of Jesus
sifts through the substance of mine; I
am God, and son of God, and man. Times I feel

my very bones become so light I may
lift unnoticed above Woods's Wood and soar
in an ecstasy of being over Acres' Lake; times again

I am so dugged, so dragged, my flesh
falls granite while a fluid near congealed
settles on my heart. The Christ – frozen in flight

on the high-flung frame of his cross –
leaves me raddled in the grossest of mercies
and I walk the length of Kane's Lane, on that ridge

of grass and cress and plantain
battening down the centre, I sex my tongue
on the flesh juices of blackberries, cinch my jaws on the chalk

bitterness of sloes, certain and unsettled,
lost and found in my body, sifted through a strait
and serpentine love-lane stretched between dawn and night.

Stranger

I too have gone down into my underworld
   seeking my father, as he went down into his;
we go on believing there is the possibility
   of discovering the rich knowledge that is held

like a life in amber and that we can return
   certain of what business we should be about. Here
is the very edge of dream, this the marsh, a green miasma
   hovering above; small birds, motionless, cling

to the reeds, like terror-stricken souls. You must cross
   in your journey, broad rivers spanned
by magnificent structures; you must cross, too,
   the laboured hills of Aquitaine and the neat

villages of Picardy. Great trucks go rushing by
   to somewhere that will not concern you; you pass
cherry trees by the roadside with their blood
   fruits, leave behind you

château, auberge, the diminished whisperings
   of wars; you will pass, too, fields of sunflowers,
those astonished and childish faces lifted
   in congregation. At a great distance the rough-cast

white of the highest mountains will appear at evening
   tipped with baby-pink; folk-art in medieval hill-top chapels
will draw out tears of innocence; in the baroque theatricals
   of later overwhelming churches, ghastly saints

will be sitting in their skeletal remains, grinning from glass caskets
   like dowdy stuffed birds; they shall remain for ever silent
and joyful on their couches. When you emerge, shaken, and carrying
   the ever-heavier burden of yourself, you may seek

solace in words, for the world burns to know what news
   the deepest darkness holds, but oh how you find
the words themselves pallid and languorous, so shy
   they lurk in hidden places like the most secretive

night animals. You will survive, you know, only as long
   as you hold to the narrow footpath, speaking your father's name
as if it served as talisman and wondering, when their time comes,
   will your children too go down into their underworld, seeking.

September 8th, 2004

eine schöne, geschnitzte, Muttergottesfigur von 1514

I readied my pilgrim-sandals, my pilgrim-heart,
for Peissenberg, and for Hohenpeissenberg; still
am I suffering the castigations of an old faith
like persistent cicada-songs in the tensile heat;

drove on the steel-sharp high-roads of Germany,
pylons lifting, triple-angled crucifixes
striding over fertile ground, great trucks
articulate, impatient, and the heavy names –

Starnberg, Weilheim, Schongau – and came into your
wooden presence, your peasant and abandoning
silence; something to do, perhaps, with an old
scrubbed scullery, with hands raw and gentle, scents

of baking, hens chuckling in the yard, and you
present to me as a love-replenishing mother. Today
they have robed you in velvet solemnity, the too-big
crown on your head sitting uneasily – but I wait, touched

again by your blank staring. Miriam. Save us from the plagues
and famines of our hearts, from the ganglion aptitude
of our lives to hate. In the chapel scrolled, such names:
Fischer, Schuster, Müller... so many boys

drowned in the horror-baths of a world war. We stand
in a sunscape higher here than the planing buzzard
and across the valley lift the glistening Alps. I would make
pendants of gold for you, the best words failing,

but implore you for innocence, you Mother, rough
and unready, everyperson, reaching in unruly light,
old faithful, washer-woman, lover – pray, the mighty
still on their seats, and the rich filled full.

Miriam

She sits, this dull and somewhat plump
goodmother, loftily enthroned, bearing a too-large
gilt and jewel-encrusted crown; she is holding out

a red-ripe fruit for which the baby Jesus –
naked and solemn-faced and somewhat plump
goodbaby, and bearing too

an over-large and jewel-encrusted crown – is reaching
eagerly; new Eve; new Adam; fruit of the tree
of suffering, and what a fine story it all makes,

this Jewish girl, this
drudge and lover, the peasant hands
roughened from kiln and goat and ossuary, in whom

unlearnèd medieval innocents
found consolation while plagues, in clouds, passed
over them, but when inveigled into leading places

in long, pestiferous warfare (something like ours), they were given
as usual, the hardest and most bitter apples
for their pains.

Madonna and Child

in memoriam, Mary Josephine Deane, née Connors

8th December; the day dawns dark, a slow
rain drawling across the suburbs; one bedraggled dog
chaws at something out of a spilled bin; wind-tortured leaves
blow wet against a litter-spattered wall.
News on the radio, wars, aggression, the old
indomitable hatreds; 'Lord,' she would quote,
'you are hard on mothers...'

A graceless urbscape, with arrogant magpies
clacking at indifferent cats, and only
a winter-flowering cherry spilling blossoms
over the garden wall. Fumes from the car
hanging on thick air, I reverse onto Cypress Downs,
mother on my mind, decades of guilt and dole, and no
way through to her, no way through to me. 8th

December, I hear it again, that scream of pain
forced from a proud woman; a midwife
(eager for fags and a rutted lane towards home)
stepping on stone-tiled floors with a tsk-tsk sharpness,
holds basin, linen, the instruments of her art. Such
an inconceivable moment, and I am intimately
involved. Grey day, and cold, with the fire
of a suffering beyond my comprehension. For which,
mother, these thanks, these
decades late, these my pleas
for your forgiveness. Irish Catholic mother, fortress
besieged, Tower of Ivory, House of Gold...

December 8th, and feast-day, the word immaculate
driving her, too, from my comprehension
and my love. A dark morning, grey daylight, this winter

softened by advent calendars and cards, people
congregate at shopping centres, how many days
to Christmas? At the start of every journey, gather
nourishment, the *Irish Times*, bars of chocolate, three
perfect pink hyacinths in a white ceramic pot.

★

We were heading south, towards the low hills; Ursula
reading aloud this morning's office, the psalms,
the antiphons and aspirations.
The road above the city had a winter clarity,
the Wicklow hills redeeming
field, hedgerow and pasture; trees standing,
a spray of mud coating their trunks,
for this is quarry road,
                                        with trucks
hauling away the innards from the lumpen hills, pressing
muck into the tarmac, a misting of muck
everywhere; from branches of a diseased elm a crow,
in black cassock, grey soutane, was preaching
though in high dudgeon, to the world.
                                                    If it was father
who came out with me into the winter night,
who climbed the quarry hill to watch the stars, an icy
breathing of island darkness holding us about
yet it was she, perhaps, was held indoors
by indoor things, oven concerns, and bucket suds;
son to father, cherishing, to mother
distant and different, in a dim and dimming otherness.

                                        Over a clutch of dung
a whorl of dancing flies turns in regulated chaos
like a universe of stars. Movement of hard-hat men –
Homeric statement of yellow overalls, of warrior
boots – the revving-up of trucks, inexorable
whittling at the core of earth for the next
crude gobbets of wealth. Big
men, big-chested, certain of what they are about.

Madonna. Miriam. Mary. There are those more beautiful
who pass like caravans on a near horizon
laden with gold out of Egypt and Ophir; she
snub-nosed, brown-skinned and undernourished, wears a few
beads of coloured glass, speaks unlovely dialect;
there are homes more beautiful, porticoes
for the moderately-off, and mansion keeps
of granite stone and marble step, cool chambers; hers

a mud-brick two-roomed shape, crowded
with family, and the lower spaces shelter sheep; hers
a brushwood roof where she can sleep at night
under the silent tumultuous stars;
she weaves, prepares and grinds, she herds,
she is a drudge, hands callused and body sore;
without dowry, scarce past puberty,
and who should desire her, save the God?

★

The first town, Blessington, long street with new streets off
into neat and manifold estates. Grey forenoon,
pre-Christmas busyness, bulbs hung above the street
and wavering in the slightest breeze; commerce,
a focusing on Santa-lit big windows, banks
festooned with winter sleighs and much-loved reindeer,
people hurrying, wrapped about themselves, hasty
bonhomie and compliments of the season. We drive
through, watchful, pausing from the breathing of the psalms.

She would sit at the kitchen table,
copies piled on the parti-coloured frayed oil-cloth,
grandfather bustling in from sheds, and father
pacing the floor like a displaced animal; she would tell
over and over the pounds and shillings and pence,

tut at the spellings, and the dull
reiteration of the island girls' ordinary days,
                                        their lot
housewifery or service, the slow labouring into flesh
laden with black wools and waitingness, or their lot
exile, housewifery or service, their arms akimbo over full
breasts, hurrying into memories, nostalgia, waitingness...
and she loved them, their staring eyes, the wool
socks inside black boots, the patchwork skirts
and cardigans, and would hymn a strict
heaven before them, a catechism of purity and care,
with tiny versicles of miracle, the sun
glancing off mauve hillside heathers onto the painted
classroom walls – till she sat back at the table, and sighed,
the pencil paused from its ticking, light fading.
                                        Something
hydrangea-like about her, mop-head, lace-cap,
how it flourished with extravagance under a kindly sun
and hung its head all brown and frowsty against the soils
of winter; if you plant nails in the earthed roots
the lace-caps alter colour; and she hoarded
sorrow at her base till it grew a virtue in her, weaponry
to hurl sorrows back against a wounding world;
Madonna. Mother. Mary Jo.

                                ★

She is not dressed in satins, nor sitting idle at a prie-dieu;
the messenger, when he comes, comes
like a fox, magister of the subtlest arts
of being. Miriam was small, robust and muscular,
she sat in the dooryard, plucking chickens, the smaller
feathers irritating fingers, her smock
spattered with blood after the killing; from the far
end of the yard a goat's laughter and nearer
the pharaoh strutting of a cock; but her dark eyes
watched beyond the hen-shit; if she could not read
nor write, she held the history of the tribes

vividly in memory, could see past the blood
                    of Nahum, Samson, Abel
into the hurt and tender eyes of God; hers
an unremarkable graced dailiness, though why the Spirit
should fall on her out of the chaos she did not
understand, she did not understand.

★

Driving between low humped hills, a curved
valley and, on the right, the small and laggard stream
that will become the Slaney. Father's eager stalking
of the river's pools, how a man cleaves
to a woman, she to him, down all the bright
dark days of their togetherness. And I tune to the radio –
Vivaldi, the music such sweet bitterness, ·
                    nulla in mundo pax sincera.
I watched her in the big bedroom, Achill, she sat
before the dressing-table, her favourite
tortoiseshell-framed hand-mirror before her face;
it was something in the stillness moved me, I saw
she was watching far beyond, out the big window
across bogland towards the distant sound,
unmoving, though her lifted hand was trembling slightly;
how the souls of those who have passed come smiling
across an inner vision that strikes us numb, at times,
though restless: witnesses, to assoil the living, on the trail
the dead have passed along, and cautioning. She shivered,
suddenly, laughed towards me and said: I think
somebody has walked across my grave.

★

After one day's mongering and dole he stands
to ponder the life of a man, a Jew-boy, this day's
exorbitant samenesses, all the days like peels

82

of white wood curling in the corner of a yard;
where a stream flows down from the snow mountain
into the lake, the woman, Jew-girl, scarce past puberty,
has spread linens out over scorched grass, stands
in the shade of a tree, dreaming: of a Jew-boy, a house;
she turns, there in the gentle emptiness of the day,
laying her tunic down, moving her dark-brown body gratefully
into the lake; beautiful the movements, her hands
piling the grape-black hair at her nape, bone of her spine
enchanting as she wades in water till she stands,
waves lapping her breasts, the rose evening
breathlessly still, as he is, watching.

      She turns and her small breasts are firm
in the fading light, the flower of her navel,
the darkening delta of her maidenhair and her thighs
rising out of the water, the water
tiny golden gifts against her skin;
she stands, unabashed, a while, her hands
gentle against the stomach-flesh, and he stands,
watching; she dresses, still wet, lightened
by her bathing and he hears her voice, a soft
and animal laughter as she moves along the shore
to stand in quiet praise and be a part of it,
the dark of early night, the trees, the water.
Out in the yard tonight they will tell
tall stories, they will sing sad songs
to the night-birds, to the kindly stars; he
will be silent, hushed in himself, and wondering.

★

She is sitting on a rug, hugging herself small
inside the wind; she is beyond the fray
of family.
      Offshore the waves
swell impetuously and break
as a line of foam goes racing angularly

across the crests, the break and long-flow reaching in
along the beach. She has been reading
a murder mystery, but something – voice or gull
or sudden catch of sorrow – has her pause, and hold
the book against her breast to watch
inwards; the beauty, the enormity of the Atlantic
won't touch her there; her ganglion of nerves,
of bone and flesh and tissue holds a moment
out of the impetus as she penetrates, despite herself,
the dreadful wall that lifts always
against our littleness. I see her shudder, her eyes
recover the wild light of sea and she returns,
gratefully, to the artificial mystery.

★

As an orchid among buttercups is she, as a peach tree
among brambles in the wood; as exile
in a hostile land, as drudge among the very poor.
Sometimes the soul, swollen with the news of creation,
grows too great for the body and leads it forth
on a journey, over fruitless hillsides, across stone-ridden
uplands, in an outflow of praise and wonder. Hers, yet,
a long apprenticeship to pain, before she grows
mistress of it, and settles down to the long night.

★

Left at the filling station; you've been down this road…
Mine is a raid on memory, the needed booty –
forgiveness; how we misunderstand each other,
willfully sometimes, more usually
out of ignorance and conceit.
                              Suddenly a rabbit, colour
of milked tea but with white ankle-socks and a Christ-child
scut of the purest white; a nibbler, big-bidder,

84

delicate on the scutch-tips, and wary. We passed
the wayside grotto, Madonna, lime-white and blue-gloss,
having little to do with our passing, this stylised
bathetic woman, not mother, a place
to burn small lights, ushering prayers away
in streels of smoke. These lowroads, twisting
to the ancient laying-out of fields, dull, untaxing.

★

She moved, unnoticed, among many
in the caravanserai, road-weary, wearied too
by the not-to-be-admitted knowledge; slept
with the animals, their warmth, their comfortable
snores and shufflings in the dark;
the camel drivers were speaking quietly together
the world's gossip, and how the tetrarch
was building palaces to himself; the muleteers
in the other yard talked drunkenly, farted, argued;
games of dice, the stench of sweat and greed;
until she slipped away, beyond the dawn, into
cinnamon-coloured hills, a merlin
circling round its cry and tiny furred and frightened lives
busy amongst the rocks and scrub. The world
                    troubled, and everywhere the powerful
fattening on detritus of rioting and wars. And sat, stilled,
small and invisible on a parched slope, in need
of woman-talk and sustenance, scared of the journey done,
more scared of the journey yet to come.

Here is a man whose dreams bear fruit. And here
is Nazareth, a village without importance, and Aramaic,
a language of strange utterance; here is Miriam, betrothed,
a girl of no importance, poor, unlearned, menial, drudge.
Here is a man, Torah-observing Jew, big-handed,
scarcely-worded carpenter, and the angels visit him
in his dreams. In cases like these, they tell us, marriage
comes first and love, perhaps, comes later.

My soul extols the greatness of the Lord
and my spirit exults in God who saves me,
for he has heeded and loved the lowliness of his servant.
And see, from this day out every generation shall know me blest,
for the mightiest One has worked wonderful things for me
                                    and holy is his name.
Down all the generations his mercy swells to those who love him.
And in this way the strength of God has been made manifest:
the arrogant in the hardness of their heart have been strewn about,
and the powerful pulled from their thrones, our God
has lifted up on high those who had been degraded;
he has fed the hungry full with the best of gifts
and those who are rich have been banished empty from his sight.
Remembering the greatness of his mercy
he has come to the aid of the oppressed,
for this has been his promise from the distant past
and will be kept down all the centuries to come.

★

I was sent in with messages; there was a hum
from the two-roomed schoolhouse, her
fiefdom; without democracy, for its own good;
here she stood, mistress, the word 'mother'
would not apply. In the small hallway
there was a smell of cocoa and damp coats;
for me the embarrassment of girls, their smirks,
their implausible and whispered comments.
A sudden silence as I moved across to her desk,
chalk-marks on the blackboard, the whole puzzle
being elucidated in one of its smaller parts;
and now? after decades: the school become
a woodwork shop, become, after failure, an abandoned
husk, small dunes of wood-dust, shavings, something
banging in the breeze with mild-mannered impatience,
and only persistent island winds that come fingering
grass and nettle, rust-work, and love, long missed.

★

They had gone on beyond the city, her pains
causing her to cry out at times and he, hurt
and ignorant and distraught, led the reluctant ass
towards the shelter of hills; a low, blue-black sky,
stars sharp already as nails, a chill wind blowing;
he would lay her down among the scrub, if necessary,
the donkey-blanket beneath her, water from a stream
to help the cleansing; there would be night-birds,
jackals, perhaps, and snakes. The great howl of the ass
frightened him and he held the woman tightly
against the cruelties of shale and the unshareable pangs
of a full pregnancy. Till the gathering dark
drew them to a small fire; in the limestone hills
a cave, small shelter against the winds, and crude
half-drunk shepherds gobbing at a fire; they heard
small life-sounds, the shiftings of a flock
and she cried again, as the lost do, against the pain.

★

Out once more on the main road, Carlow / Enniscorthy;
I eased my grip on the wheel; a truck
sent up a spray of dirtied rain as I sped past;
I remember thinking how much I love the woman
quiet beside me on this searing trip. Mount Leinster
invisible in the gathered mists, this rich-soil land
fallow and puddled in the Irish winter. Slaney
broader now, its dark flow soiled with a factory's
olive outspill, and trees being hacked out of the way
for some no-doubt necessary building. I reached,
touching the woman's hand, for presence, reassurance, warmth.

★

Walnuts, figs; the tiniest hairs of the gooseberry;
she would touch the sap of balsam trees
to her children's skin, cure headache and weeping eyes;
she would rub docken leaves where the sting of nettles
scalded. Morning, the jacaranda tree letting go
its misty dreaming, it could be again the outset of the world
where man and animal stand astonished; under the dreeping bush
she sets out, deep-breathing, to take her place before the class;
her children brought to task, the strange one
hungry at the carpenter's desk; there is poverty, taxation, a little
beggary, and at times her own unruly sons
pestering the neighbours; she prepares a barley porridge,
for supper there will be cucumbers, onions, nuts and oranges;
on each fourth Sabbath, with luck, a salted fish; potato bread and farl,
cabbage cooked in bacon stock, thick and smoked rasher slices;
on Fridays herring, in Lent one meal and two collations.

★

And then we were slowing down the long hill
into Bunclody; a varied shrubbery, the small town
laying itself out below; a soft-toned town, to retire to.
I ease the car to a halt, opposite the bungalow, memories
like exhaust fumes stirring through the heavy air; there
the plants he nursed, soil he laboured; that window
was her room, her privacy, her prayer-time, ministries;
blank now, reflecting this bleak day, and unresponding.
After her death, the house loud with visitors, I slept
alone in her room and in her bed; the moon sent a dull,
pre-Christmas light through the curtains; I knew, at last,
a weight of sadness, a slow welling of loss; a scent
remained, her talcs and creams, the dressing-table things,
a glass tea-tray for rings and hairpins, and there
in the empty hours after dawn, I saw
her tortoiseshell hand-mirror, dusted,
and a crinkled prayer-card to Saint Anthony, patron
of all lost things. Mother. Who has taken away with her
her bundles of sufferings, inflated anxieties

for her children's souls, and every possibility
of mutual understanding and forgiveness.
                                    On then,
the river again on our left, through the rich and fallow fields
till we drew up, at last, by the graveyard wall
under dripping trees. That certain pause, a small
silence, and then the gathering of coats, umbrellas,
the pot with its three pink hyacinths. The car doors
closed, startling through the almost stillness of the rain,
intrusive ping-song of the automatic lock, and then,
destination, the rising recurrent sorrow of the merely
human before loss, its unacceptability, its disdain.

★

8th December. 1943.
The world was stretched
feverish under war. There was a fall
of snow, they told me, over the heathlands.
Achill. My island. Call me
John. After the Evangelist. And Francis, after the poor
and love-tossed fool. And call me
Mary, for the day that's in it, and for mother, worn
after the pain and tearing. There were men
wading through an underworld of blood and muck
uncomprehending. I hear the winter storms
crying through the pine grove. Mother. Mary.
Mother and son. Madonna. A winter child.

★

After it all, after all this, the years, the distances,
after the days and absences and angers, what can I do
but stand in stillness by the grave, her name
and his, only a dream breeze touching
the trees and a soft rain falling? Stand,

nothing to say, all said, winter, and grey,
my presence I hope amounting to something,
to sorrow, pleading, the three pink hyacinths.
I step across her grave to lay them by the headstone,
offering a presence more eloquent than mine.
                    Mother again, and child,
the light along the body is olive green; I wonder
if they would have draped him across her knees? The blood,
the gore, the fluids. I wonder if she even had
that much comfort? This loved and cared-for body
torn now, reviled; that she bore and birthed
in anxiety and sorrow; God's abandonment of him
is doubly hers. And can you hear them all, the women?
Mothers, daughters, sisters… their cries
across time and space, joining with her in ongoing silence
that shatters the world across every century,
crying against war and killing, against crucifixion, torture, rape,
the fact of the disappeared, the pulling down of love.

The Jesus Body, the Jesus Bones

Supposing the God to be moody and resentful
he has made us yet – earthen vessels of spittle and clay – in likeness
of himself, longing to crucify and to be
crucified. Once I danced, my girl-child born,

on deserted streets, the way God must have danced across his vast
echoing ballroom, everything now poised
to begin; but we begin, and begin again. Homes, up
beyond their eaves in flood-water, lie still

as ranked coffins after war, corpses
floating, ceiling-high. This is a bleak and weakening framework
of streets and intersections,
basements, hallways, embarrassed kitchens, slumped

like the fluid
interstices of the brain. How the mind, receiving warnings, will slew
away, unwilling. After the first flood,
God's stir of bitterness appeased, a silence moved over the waters;

do poplars breathe or hold for forty days
their breathing? and raptors, do they soar so high and live on dreams
for forty nights? We have lain,
fallen into earth, and softening. This evening

on the slow hills, such downpour-music, such culvert-chords, such
drain-strings; the rooks, vested in solemn black,
announce their raucous vespers; rains have ended, the tipsy
fingers jittering at our windows

ceased, and in the after-loneliness
moths that had tangoed to the candles' flames grew precious
for the brevity of their hours. At last
high and lumbering things, elephant, emu and giraffe

came cautiously out into the air
from the rough-wood ribs of the Ark, woodlice and earwigs
in quick-step from the mud; all animal things
stepped, as perhaps each dawn they do or every dusk, astonished

at the washed aspect of the world.
Within our bones the folded feathers and frame of a grateful spirit
wait and sulk, that will lift one day
with the potency of resurrection out over the muddied earth.

The Jesus Body

Triduum

I had been reading Dante and was shaken once again
how we suffer appalling punishment for being human;
I stepped out to breathe awhile in the good air.

After yesterday's excess this sacred Saturday was still;
adult hares played in the wild meadow; across the hedgerow
ash and larch broke against the skyline, but all I saw was the Christ

with his contained sufferings, stride down the laneways of Sheol
calling aloud redemption. I almost stepped on a baby hare
crouched low and coloured as the dun rushes, dying, it seemed,

the eyes glazed over. It was a long day, sluggish with vague
expectations, and the long night dark and untenanted. Morning,
when I carried out the ashes, finch and wren and robin

washed the hedgerows with a rioting of song; and suddenly
the baby hare! Insolent, nibbling the edges of new growth
on the fern till I clapped my hands, impatient against such

disturbance, and it glanced at me, and slowly loped away.

The Jesus Body

There was a child...

found a nest of stones by the lakeshore, fire-blackened, fish
bones, fish
scales; material to interpret, a passing
of something, unnamed, and dangerous;

around the house they whispered it, a visitant
testing family borders. There was a child, they taught me,
in Nazareth, indolent, perhaps, like me,
remote in place and nature; yet he

was sedulous with timber in a workshop, time and purpose
falling in curlicues about his feet. The first
wonder, this tumbling out of nowhere
onto time. I moved through days in a pact of ignorance

with rock and breeze and water till a fox
barked suddenly from its place of secrecy and I tipped
startled, into a small
guilt; and often still, a pain within will catch me,

suddenly, in the pit, here. There was a den, in the drip of rain
off heathers, a mouth into uncanny earth;
hen-feathers, a small treasury of sucked bones; and even yet,
in the taut distress of sleepless nights,

at home, or in the restlessness for home, across alien geographies
of airports or the brusque indifference of adequate
hotels, the child in me will hear
the remonstrating barking of a fox. Grandfather, dusk,

solemnly wound his big fob watch,
and the standing-clock, and the loud-ticked mantel clock;
small beads of moisture
gathered on the yellowing ends of his moustache; his footsteps

came sounding out of the nineteenth century; tick,
and tock, and tick, and tock. I rummaged
in his carpenter's shed, hiding sometimes
in the wooden-bodied fragrant grain-bin, pulling a roof of darkness

down over my misbehaving; but often it was
wistfulness at windows, the pointlessness and unasking
sadnesses of a child. A time I held
the iron key to the chapel door; there was frosted glass

furze-blossom gold; Jesus on his niche, child-out-of-shape,
one hand begging alms, the eyes
fastened to a world beyond the known; I was floating then
on a dark ocean and came ashore

– egret or avocet or loon – on the marble altar, fascinated
by the seasonal colours of vestments, by tasselled bookmarks and all
that weight of Latin. Down in the village a cock crowed
warmth and sunlight; a dog was yowling

for shame of its mongrelhood; the angelus bell
scattered dust across the air while that strange and remote child Jesus
was made into flesh again, the earth transformed (we bent
our knee to the ground) time

glowing from within with eternal purposes. Later I knelt
by grandfather in the pew, proud to be on the men's side;
he kept nudging me to
kneel up straight, stop fidgeting; I was looking up

at Jesus' face to see if his eyes moved, if he fidgeted
out of his stiffness. And then, one afternoon
father's car drew up alongside on the road; excited
I was hopping up down, up down, that

pendulum irritation, on the running-board till he told me
grandfather has died. I sat
in the back seat and assumed, for the first time,
solemnity; there were clay pipes for the waking, cold beef sandwiches

and whiskey softening the consonants of old men.
Jesus, the stranger, became a lurking
presence in the dark inglenook; daffodils under the trees, forced
daffodils in the vase, that heavy scent of spring

since then suggesting death and that golden yellow glow
the pallor of our dying. In Nazareth
they drink the wine of dread; in a sunlit street a car
has been torn asunder, the tyres burning, small

trenches of black blood pooling, and women,
kerb-side, sharpening their anguish, their hands
raised pleading to the alien cameras.
Grandfather lies alone in his earth bed, part of the ordering of time

that is drawing coverlets of moss and grasses over him;
above his name, faded too, a face of Jesus
wretched in a wreathe of thorns. And day by day the slow
dandelion clocks blow gently on the winds that cross the world.

The Final Prayer

I stand before him and he says
'Body of Christ' and I chew on flesh, he says
'Blood of Christ' and I taste a bitter, small inebriation;
I take the substance deep into my substance and can say
I, too, am Jesus; and I pray
(thanks to the Jesus body, the Jesus bones)
that the deaf will hear the breezes
siffling through the eucalyptus trees
and the breaking of waves along Atlantic's shingle shores,
that the blind, after darkness and the shadows that darkness throws,
will see the moonlight play like fireflies
along the undersides of leaves,
that those of us botched in brain and limb will be
gazelles across an intimate terrain and that the tears
of the too-old woman, inward-dwelling, wheelchair-locked
who lost her lover-man to death some twenty years ago
will step out giddily again
into blue erotic light.